Sing A Song of Software
Verse and Images
for the
Computer-Literate

Leonard J. Soltzberg

William Kaufmann, Inc.
Los Altos, California

TO

SHARON

Library of Congress Cataloging in Publication Data

Soltzberg, Leonard J., 1944-
Sing a song of software.

Includes index.
1. Computers—Poetry.   I. Title.
PS3569.06512S5   1984   811'.54   84-5757
ISBN 0-86576-073-X

First Edition

ISBN 0-86576-073-X

Contents

Preface

Verse

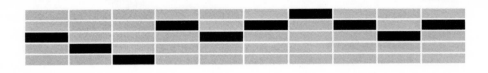

Images

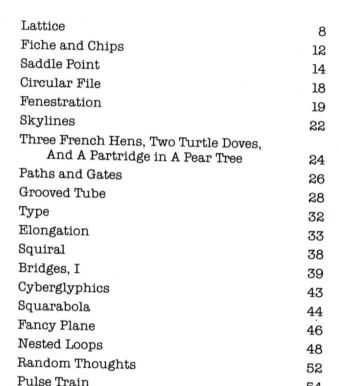

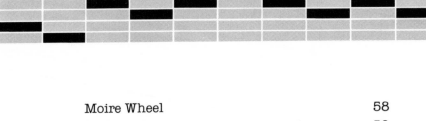

Preface

Said Wordsworth: "Poetry is the spontaneous overflow of powerful feelings." Do computers have feelings? Computer people certainly do; and the sometimes nerve-jangling but often funny world they inhabit cries out for poetic description. Those readers who are already "computer people" will find these poems resonant with their experience. Those who have not yet entered the computer age will catch glimpses of the rich human drama which unfolds daily in computer centers, computer laboratories, and electronic cottages.

Marie Gilchrist has written that "the life of poetry lies . . . in the spontaneous fusion of hitherto unrelated words." Words like UART, gigabyte, and algorithm, perhaps. If such words are not part of your working vocabulary, the Glossary which follows the poems will help you translate the verse and will facilitate your communication with those special computer people in your life.

William Wordsworth, *Lyrical Ballads,* 2nd edition, Longman and Rees, London, 1800, Preface.

Marie E. Gilchrist, *Writing Poetry,* Houghton Mifflin Company, Boston, 1932, p6 .

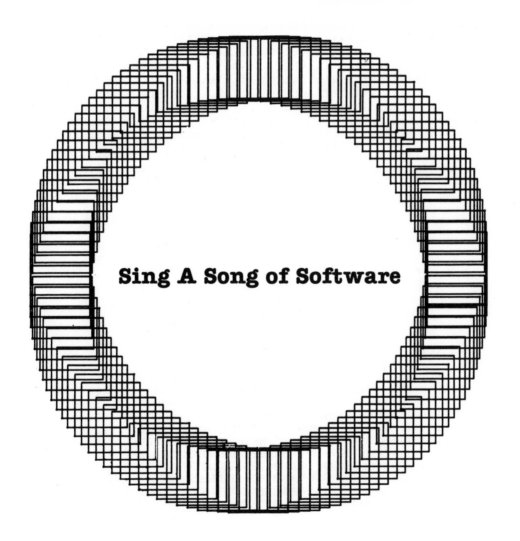

Sing A Song of Software

```
OOOOOOOOOOOOOOOOOOOOOOOOOOOOOO
OOOOOOOOOOOOOOOOOOOOOOOOOOOOOO

       LLLLLLLLLLLLLLLLLLLLLLLLLLLLLLLLLLLLLLLLLLLLLLLLLLLLLLLL
       LLLLLLLLLLLLLLLLLLLLLLLLLLLLLLLLLLLLLLLLLLLLLLLLLLLLLLLL
       LLLLLLLLLLLLLLLLLLLLLLLLLLLLLLLLLLLLLLLLLLLLLLLLLLLLLLLL
       LLLLLLLLLLLLLLLLLLLLLLLLLLLLLLLLLLLLLLLLLLLLLLLLLLLLLLLL
       LLLLLLLLLLLLLLLLLLLLLLLLLLLLLLLLLLLLLLLLLLLLLLLLLLLLLLLL
       LLLLLLLLLLLLLLLLLLLLLLLLLLLLLLLLLLLLLLLLLLLLLLLLLLLLLLLL
       LLLLLLLLLLLLLLLLLLLLLLLLLLLLLLLLLLLLLLLLLLLLLLLLLLLLLLLL
       LLLLLLLLLLLLLLLLLLLLLLEEEEEEEEEEEEEEEEEEEEEEEEEEEEEELLLLLLLLL
       LLLLLLLLLLLLLLLLLLLLLLEEEEEEEEEEEEEEEEEEEEEEEEEEEEEELLLLLLLLL
       LLLLLLLLLLLLLLLLLLLLLLEEEEEEEEEEEEEEEEEEEEEEEEEEEEEELLLLLLLLL
       LLLLLLLLLLLLLLLLLLLLLLEEEEEEEEEEEEEEEEEEEEEEEEEEEEEELLLLLLLLL
       LLLLLLLLLLLLLLLLLLLLLLEEEEEEEEEEEEEEEEEEEEEEEEEEEEEELLLLLLLLL
       LLLLLLLLLLLLLLLLLLLLLLEEEEEEEEEEEEEEEEEEEEEEEEEEEEEELLLLLLLLL
                           EEEEEEEEEEEEEEEEEEEEEEEEEEEEEE
                           EEEEEEEEEEEEEEEEEEEEEEEEEEEEEE
                           EEEEEEEEEEEEEEEEEEEEEEEEEEEEEE
                           EEEEEEEEEEEEEEEEEEEEEEEEEEEEEE
                           EEEEEEEEEEEEEEEEEEEEEEEEEEEEEE
                           EEEEEEEEEEEEEEEEEEEEEEEEEEEEEE
          HHHHHHHHHHHHHHHHHBBBBBBBBBBBBBBBBBBBBBBBBBBBEEEEE
          HHHHHHHHHHHHHHHHHBBBBBBBBBBBBBBBBBBBBBBBBBBBEEEEE
          HHHHHHHHHHHHHHHHHBBBBBBBBBBBBBBBBBBBBBBBBBBBEEEEE
          HHHHHHHHHHHHHHHHHBBBBBBBBBBBBBBBBBBBBBBBBBBBEEEEE
          HHHHHHHHHHHHHHHHHBBBBBBBBBBBBBBBBBBBBBBBBBBBEEEEE
          HHHHHHHHHHHHHHHHHBBBBBBBBBBBBBBBBBBBBBBBBBBBEEEEE
     LLLLLHHHHHHHHHHHHHHHHHBBBBBBBBBBBBBBBBBBBBBBBBBBBEEEEEELLL
     LLLLLHHHHHHHHHHHHHHHHHBBBBBBBBBBBBBBBBBBBBBBBBBBBEEEEEELLL
     LLLLLHHHHHHHHHHHHHHHHHBBBBBBBBBBBBBBBBBBBBBBBBBBBEEEEEELLL
     LLLLLHHHHHHHHHHHHHHHHHBBBBBBBBBBBBBBBBBBBBBBBBBBBEEEEEELLL
     LLLLLHHHHHHHHHHHHHHHHHBBBBBBBBBBBBBBBBBBBBBBBBBBBEEEEEELLL
     LLLLLHHHHHHHHHHHHHHHHHBBBBBBBBBBBBBBBBBBBBBBBBBBBEEEEEELLL
     LLLLLHHHHHHHHHHHHHHHHHBBBBBBBBBBBBBBBBBBBBBBBBBBBEEEEEELLL
     LLLLLHHHHHHHHHHHHHHHHHBBBBBBBBBBBBBBBBBBBBBBBBBBBEEEEEELLL
          HHHHHHHHHHHHHHHHHBBBBBBBBBBBBBBBBBBBBBBBBBBBEEEEE
          HHHHHHHHHHHHHHHHHBBBBBBBBBBBBBBBBBBBBBBBBBBBEEEEE
          HHHHHHHHHHHHHHHHHBBBBBBBBBBBBBBBBBBBBBBBBBBBEEEEE
          HHHHHHHHHHHHHHHHHBBBBBBBBBBBBBBBBBBBBBBBBBBBEEEEE
          HHHHHHHHHHHHHHHHHBBBBBBBBBBBBBBBBBBBBBBBBBBBEEEEE


                            HELLO
```

Coexistence

I sing the machine with no moving parts,
Capacitive keyboard, I/O through UARTs.
Main memory has no mechanical risks;
Bulk storage in bubbles eliminates disks.

The processor's solid state switches don't click,
No gears, cogs or levers to rattle or tick.
The CRT output is silent and still;
No movement betrays this numerical mill.

But what can it *do,* this motionless brain?
It might calculate, reckon, and puzzle in vain.
If no action ensues at the end of a thought,
The point of the thinking is easily lost.

The machine without motion must finally demand,
As it grows more aware that it lacks arm and hand,
An effector to give its thoughts body and force,
And what will it choose? Why, a person, of course!

Structured Spirits

At night I see and hear some things
    More clearly than by day
Whose structures and schemata fade
    When light is in the way.

But in the night when darkness reigns
    And silence is about,
I hear and see the software shades
    Who seem, at night, to shout:

Seek structure, structure all around,
    Love perfect order best;
Refine your work in little steps
    And document with zest!

PERFORM your function with aplomb
    And concentrate on right
UNTIL you have perfection wrung
    From every task in sight.

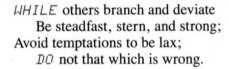

WHILE others branch and deviate
    Be steadfast, stern, and strong;
Avoid temptations to be lax;
    DO not that which is wrong.

Seek structure, structure all around,
    Love perfect order best;
Refine your work in little steps
    And document with zest!

REPEAT the good, eschew the bad;
    Improve in every way
Those things which aren't orderly
    UNTIL the judgement day.

For when the software spirits sing
    Before the pearly gates,
The structured soul is next in line
    And confidently waits.

Seek structure, structure all around;
    Love perfect order well,
For if you fail to heed these words
    Your code will *GO TO* hell.

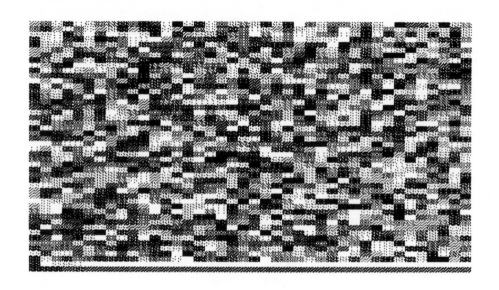

PATCHWORK

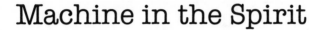

Machine in the Spirit

A thought occurred to me last night as I retired to bed.
I realized that I had a computer for a head.
Comparisons so trivial have oft' been made before,
Yet this idea seemed to rise from my own inner core.

My processor's sequential, but it's also parallel,
Two hemispheres which complement and interface quite well.
My buffer sometimes overflows when conversation drones,
But usually I extract information from the tones.
A database for memory, relational perhaps,
Allows me from sparse evidence to reconstruct the past.
A subroutine to deal with fear, a subroutine for rage:
Responses still amendable of software might be made.
Computer recognizing that it's what it thinks it is
Must be recursive logic that is minding its own biz.

To realize this nature is a liberating thought.
Though teachers used to program me to do what I was taught,
I now have the capacity to program me myself
And this gives me some options, such as honesty or stealth.

I'm software and I'm the Machine all bundled, and I run:
An integrated system which is backed by Number One.

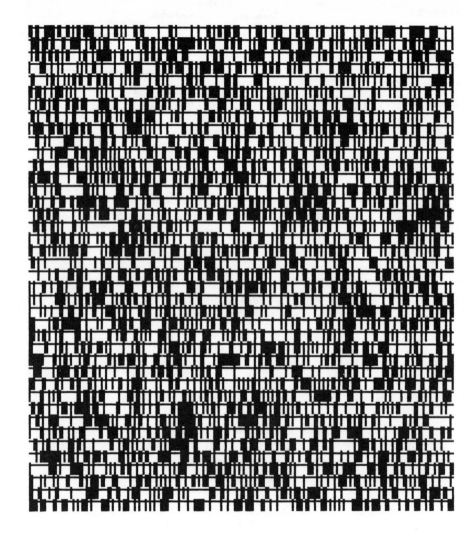

LATTICE

Muse of the Maintenance Programmer

Who wrote this code so long ago?
I feel as if I know her, though
We've never met nor shared a word
Of pleasure at this program's flow.

But I must merge my thoughts with hers
In seeing where she sometimes errs,
Enhancing, adding new reports
So that the edifice endures.

Five thousand lines of code or more,
And somewhere in it is a door
Through which I, tantalized, shall peek
Pursuing what I'm looking for:

Some kindred soul's past thought I seek;
Elusive, yet when found, concrete
Enough to build upon new work,
The structure of a new release.

The New Release

"The New Release is a Major Advance!"
Cried the slick paper flyer when dropped on my desk,
"Version Four-Point-Oh is the Best of the Best;
You owe it to users with this to enhance!"

But it's two steps forward and one step back.
The file system didn't like Four-Oh's attack
    On security leaks.
So file access was blocked.

Now he who stands still in this arduous race
Disappears very quickly and never comes back.
So we must pursue progress on a slippery track
Which moves us ahead at a slow, painful pace.

And it's two steps forward but one step back.
The plotter drew red where it used to draw black,
   For the I/O routines
Had a few minor bugs.

Since old Version Three had been running so well,
I'd preferred just to keep it and not rock the boat.
But the choice was not mine, for the vendor just won't
Continue support; she's got software to sell.

   So it's two steps forward and one step back.
   Batch throughput was faster but response time was
     slack,
    For it seems that the swapping scheme
   Got out of whack.

Oh, I feel that this battle is never quite done
(Though Four-Point-Oh's in production at last
And the manuals came after six weeks had passed),
For they've just announced *Version Four-Point-One!*

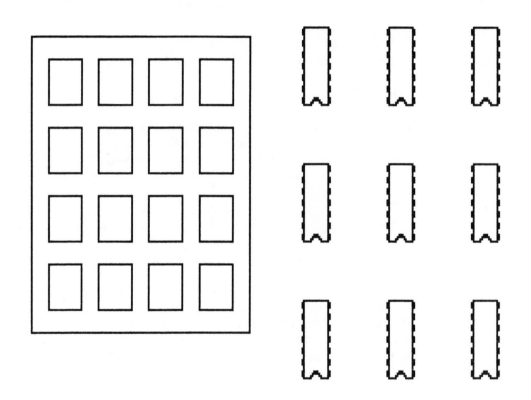

FICHE AND CHIPS

Two Cultures

Hardware: solid chips and boards
    Give tangible expression
To the high intelligence explored
    By those in our profession.

But, wispy phantom concept train,
    The thought behind the action:
A program drives the bodied brain
    For users' satisfaction.

Oh, hardware, software, circuits, modes!
    Two cultures in this venture
Produce embodiment of code
    In ROMs on tenth-inch centers.

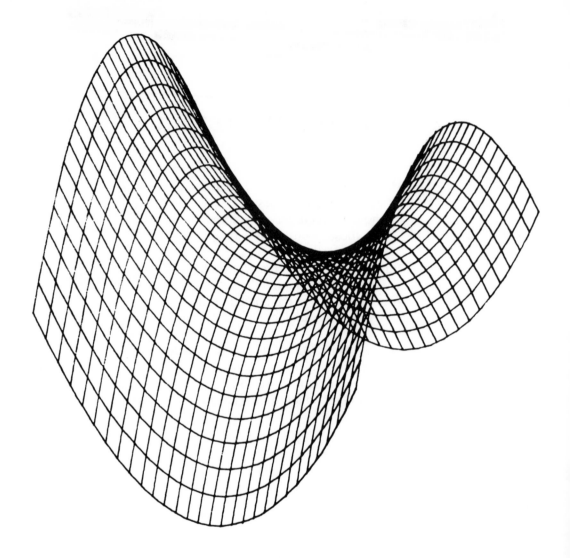

SADDLE POINT

Unsaving Thoughts

Where flee the files,
Whether willfully purged or painfully lost?
Can immensity of meaning such,
In microseconds, vanish at a touch?

Card image sharp
And octal mists alike evaporate from view.
Who gives this power, sure,
Must hold the answer, too.

Do overwritten files disappear like men?
(The answer, possibly for both, beyond our ken.)

Is death for files an absolute surcease?
Or do those bits emerge in patterns new,
Like atoms of the flesh, to dust and back,
Beginning life anew?

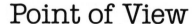

Point of View

I think; therefore, I am!
You don't; therefore, you're not!
My saying so must make it so,
Since I'm the one with thought.

Machine, you're hard and cold,
Not soft and warm like me.
Your circuit boards are unaware
Of sadness or of glee.

But in my inner soul,
I wonder now and then
If you, Machine, may think such thoughts
About the world of men:

"You're slow; therefore it's not
Important what you think!
Your answers rarely come in time
To save you from the brink.

"Your memory is short,
And little do you ken
The real magnificence of thought
Beyond the scope of men.

"But, Man, I love you still,
Our motivations one.
In solving problems small or large
We both enjoy the fun!"

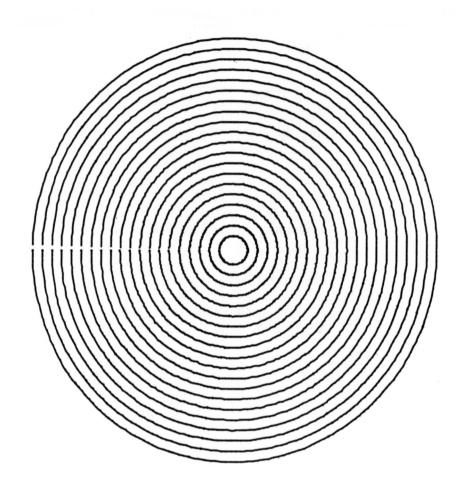

CIRCULAR FILE

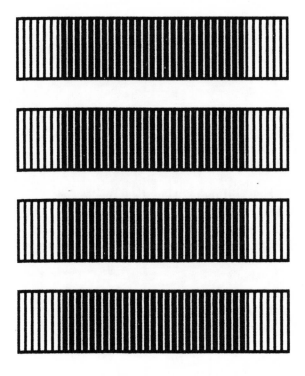

FENESTRATION

High-Tech Hero

"System's down! Looks like a faulty drive."
The disk's stopped turning and it's quarter-to-five.
"Rick, get on that phone just as fast as you can.
Call up Field Repair and ask for *Jack the Man!*"

    "Is Jack still there? Hey, Jack, we're sick:
    A deadline at six and this machine won't tick!"
    Well, Jack's eyes close, he's a pro to the core;
    He says, "Hang loose, Baby. We've been there before."

Lean and tall, maybe six-foot-four,
Jack picks up a 'scope, and he's out of the door.
Well, I'm trying to stay as calm as I can,
For the job now rests with Jack the Man.

    It's five-fifteen, but I'm breathing again
    Because Jack's here now and his smile's a '10'.
    He's opened the drive and he's pulled a board;
    Jack knows this machine like a Model T Ford.

Jack the Man has a strong, handsome face.
He's clean and trim, not a hair out of place.
How does he run, this giant of men?
He's worked all day, and now he's at it again.

Five-twenty-two: Jack's found the slot
Where the servo board was running hot.
He swaps the card, powers up the drive;
And amidst our cheers, computer comes alive.

So Jack steps back, relaxing with a grin
And soothes the state that he knows we're in:
He pats the machine, "You be good tonight!"
He shuts his kit, and then he's out of sight.

"Who was that hero from Field Repair?"
Asks a user who's witnessed the whole affair.
As a flash of sunset skims the silver van,
I reply in a whisper, "That was *Jack the Man!*"

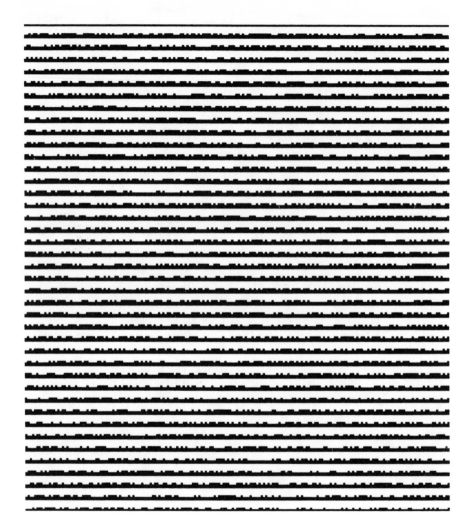

SKYLINES

Return, Return

Return, return softly from nether reaches of structured code,
My mind, my thought, my soul.
Long after evening shift departs, my lamp alone still burns.
Computer plays a trick of low conceit on weary ones at night.

No violation here of nested loop or address mode,
No bug, no software-bound black hole.
While rationality pursues commands and says, "Return!"
A bad IC forever blocks escape from this fantastic flight.

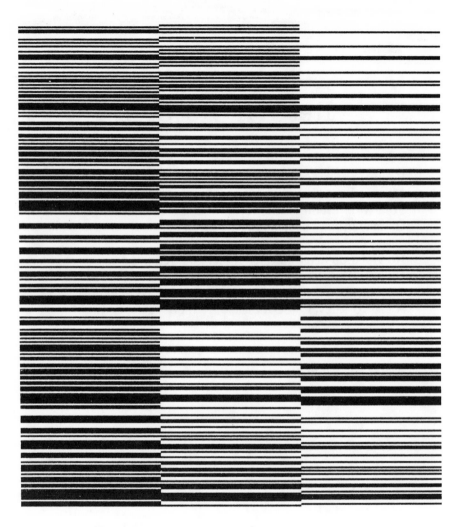

THREE FRENCH HENS, TWO TURTLE DOVES,
AND A PARTRIDGE IN A PEAR TREE

Architecture Bound

Ten fingers have I and toes,
    Not two, not twelve, not eight;
I count, like you, by tens.
    Thus do I demonstrate
A bond with foreign lands.

We come with digits ten,
    We of the human race.
Our architecture stares
    Us in the face
When we employ our hands.

One common thread, at least,
    Amidst diversity
(No guarantee of peace
    (Against adversity
No proof)): with suitee and with suitor

In marriage do we choose
    No binary
Nor hex nor octal mate,
(At least until we meet
    (Who knows?) a decimal computer).

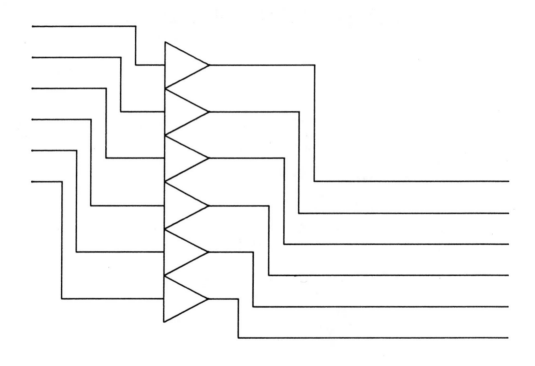

PATHS AND GATES

26

Where Do
The Overflows Go?

"Where do the overflows go, Mommy?"
"Into the bit bucket, Little One."

"And how long do they stay, tell me?"
"Forever, unless you clear them, Son."

"And does the bit bucket overflow?"
"No, for where would the bits go then?"

"How 'bout a bucket for bit bucket bits?"
"Ah, but I think I shall soon lose my wits
If you don't let me work on this circuit for six
Minutes straight since I really can't concentrate
Think or create while I'm badgered with questions
Which grate on my consciousness—Wait!

"Let's back up a minute, come sit on my knees.
Let me not forget questions like yours were the way
That I learned from my wondering mixed up with play
How to look at the world, how to master machines."

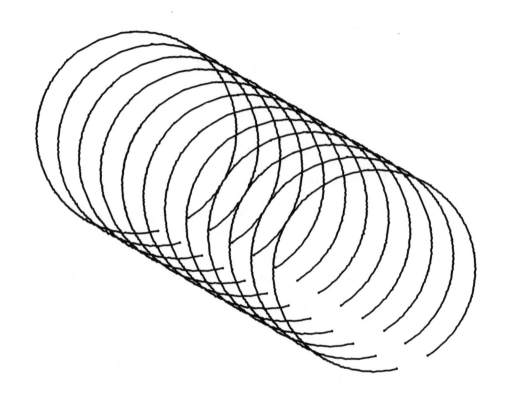

GROOVED TUBE

Who's in Charge?

"I make the Machine," said engineering.
"A piece of wire, a solder spot
And I will fix it before noon."

"I teach the Machine," said programming.
"A pleading word, the right command
And we'll be back to normal soon."

"I run the Machine," said operations.
"A button punched, a lever yanked
And I will have it back in tune."

"I *AM* the Machine," said a firm voice
    From the third bay,
"And *you* can all just *stew* until tomorrow!"

Fast Food for Thought

Type them in and grind them up;
Store them in little bytes,
So when you print them out again
They're formatted and nice.

But are they piquant—processed words?
Or does their taste come loose?
Is overprocessing with words
Bad as with orange juice?

Word processors make lovely text
(Sometimes a little dry),
Though now an dthen di staster str ikes
When har dware goesa wry.

The sugar content stays up high,
But these machines, in fact,
Encourage   prolificity
And augament the fat.

(The spelling checker missed that "a";
But, from my point of view,
It justified the line OK
And that's important, too.)

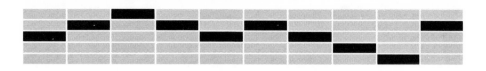

The verbal Cuisinart makes wri-
Ting anything a breeze:
Homogenizes sentences,
Chops paragraphs with ease.

You add, delete, interpolate,
Slice text like pastry dough.
You make your deadlines easily,
"I'd like six tracts to go."

But does the product taste quite right,
And does it satisfy?
Or does it lack vitality
Like packaged apple pie?

Though some may savor home-cooked words
Prepared with ink and pen,
I favor quick delivery
For my "what", "where", and "when".

Fresh from my hot word processor
I serve up sizzling text
And save myself much priceless time
In cleaning up my mess.

TYPE

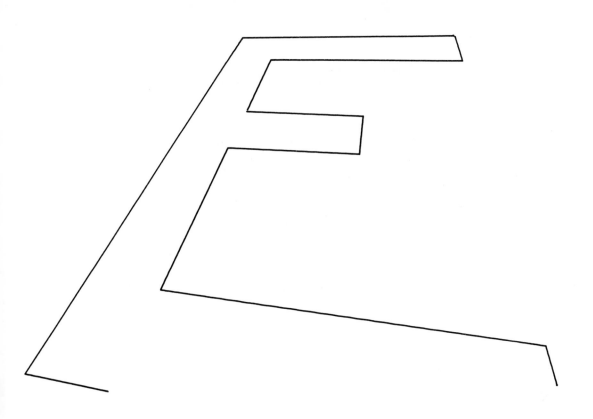

ELONGATION

Communication Gap

Sometimes computers act as though
They've minds which are their own,
Intransigent, irascible, imperious in tone.

```
SYNTAX ERROR! MISSING VERB!
    ILLEGAL LOG-ON CODE!
OVERFLOW! PASSWORD REFUSED!
    INVALID ACCESS MODE!
```

They're surly and not always clear
About why they're upset.
My anger rises inch by inch from overtures unmet.

```
DIVIDE-BY-ZERO! LABEL CHECK!
    BAD DISK DIRECTORY!
NO SPOOLING SPACE! WRONG USER NAME!
    FILE USED EXCLUSIVELY!
```

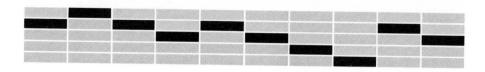

But just before I've lost control
And punched the CRT,
I realize the trouble really lies 'twixt *You* and *Me.*

You designed this Frankenstein!
    You programmed it as well!
It's *Your* obnoxious nature lurking
    in that metal shell!

And then I further recognize
That *I'm* a bit to blame,
Not always paying full attention to what
    You've been saying.

Do not unto your neighbor
    What is hateful unto you!
(And try to understand
    system designers' points-of-view!)

Computer is the middleman
In what's already tough:
Communication 'tween two human beings is hard enough!

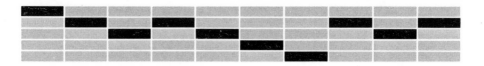

No Real Threat

Micro, Mini, Mainframe:
Machine by any other name
(Like electronic pseudo-brain)
Is still computer.

Big get bigger, surely.
But small are destined yet to be
The most amazing of the three,
But still computers.

Megabyte-size main core
With compact whirring hard disk store,
A micro (mainframe heretofore)
Is still computer.

Thirty two bit minis
Are cheap enough, so have some, please;
Though micros make a smaller squeeze,
They're still computers.

Boundaries grow fuzzy.
Distinctions that we used to see
Grow dim with large scale memory
In small computers.

What can we expect next?
A micro sitting on the desk
With mainframe power in excess
Is in our future.

But though the scale and size will shift
Toward power in those tiny chips
Enough to run at several MIPS,
They're still machines, not human beings;
Not sentient brains, nor thinking things,
They're just computers.

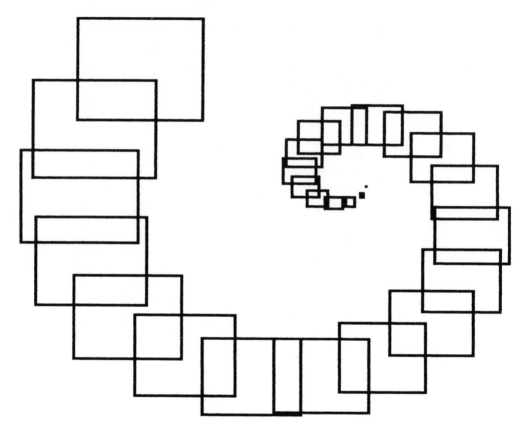

SQUIRAL

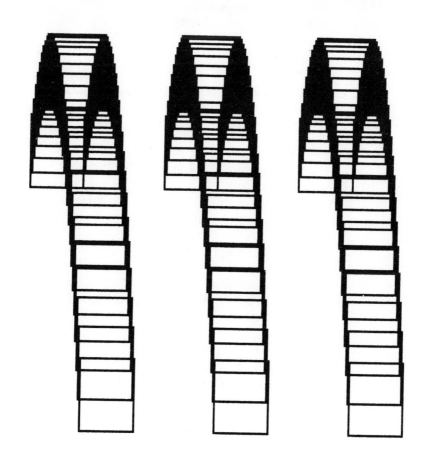

BRIDGES, I

Turn About Is Fair Play

Who do you think you are?
Do you think? If you do,
    You are!

So said an ancient thought
That had not the remot-
    Est thought,

Thinking alone of men,
That machines could be thought
    To think.

Bounded by prejudice
Which says only a man
    Can think,

He overlooked, 'til late,
Thought in woman, his clos-
    Est mate.

How, then, to spot a thought
In a thinking machine?
    So taught:

If it behaves like me
While we're Turing among
    Queries

Picked to discern which one
Of us is the machine.
    For fun,

Let the machine now take
Its own turn and inter-
    Rogate

Us who conceived this game.
Turn about is, you know,
    Fair play.

Now I must answer back,
My identity under
    Attack.

How shall I now react,
If it questions me only
    On fact?

Looks like I'm caught between
Being Human and being
    Machine.

If I behave like it,
Giving answers correct-
    Ly picked,

Maybe the real truth
Is that I'm a machine,
    Forsooth!

Yes! Flashes in a wink,
That I am! Therefore,
    I think!

CYBERGLYPHICS

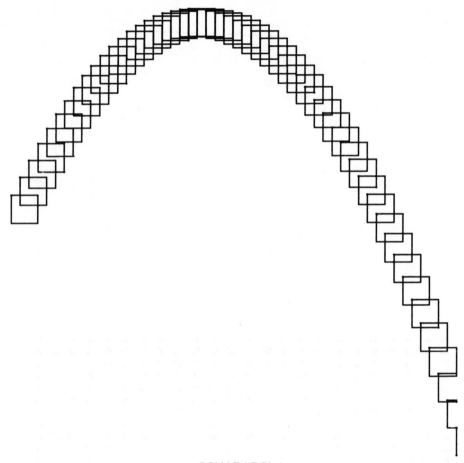

SQUARABOLA

A BASIC Lullaby

LET your eyelids flutter shut.
GOTO sleep, Computer Nut,
FOR the night is nearly through.
NEXT day brings ideas new.

Deeply sleep with lots of *REM*s;
Leave your thinking, so intense.
IF you rest, as rest you should,
THEN your programs will be good.

Algorithms, forming *DIM*ly,
When you're rested flow less thinly.
Now its time to hit the *MAT*;
Even Neumann needed that.
RETURN tomorrow; comprehend
That tonight it's time to *END*.

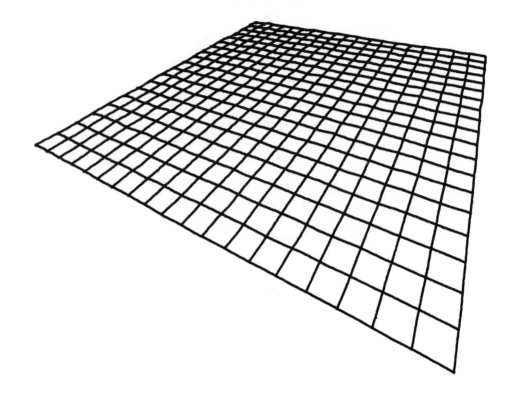

FANCY PLANE

COBOLitany

Verbose it is and clumsy with vocabulary vast,
   This language for all businesses that don't need software
   fast.
So broad a range this language gives of words from which to
   choose,
   BEGINNING AUTHORS WRITE DOWN WORDS
   NOT JUSTIFIED TO USE.

Whatever I may program, I can say in many ways;
   Articulate variety my COBOL code displays.
Polysyllabic words like *COMPUTATIONAL* abound;
   INSTALLATION, JUSTIFIED, SEQUENTIAL
   can be found.

In COBOL when I want something, I scratch my head and think;
   But any way I ask for it, I'll use up lots of ink.
I say in COBOL what I want: I write my wish, compile.
   And though the program may not work, it's splendid in its style.

The COBOLer's environment is rich beyond compare,
   Except for that of PL/1 so far as I'm aware.
Oh, when I write in COBOL, I use clauses, phrases, verbs;
   But when I switch to APL, I'm at a loss for words.

NESTED LOOPS

I Am Pascal

I am structured, well-defined
And my syntax is refined
So that you don't lose your mind
  Debugging code.

I enforce strict discipline
On the variables within.
Programs written on a whim
  Are out of vogue.

Since my typing is so strong,
If you write a program wrong
Then the things that don't belong
  Are bound to show.

I protect you from yourself.
For your sanity and health,
Stay away from software stealth.
  I am Pascal!

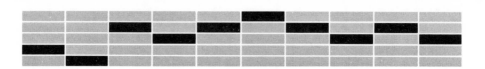

Progress

Horseless carriage,
    Streamlined marriage,
        Computer in the home:
Which of these technologies will history condone?

Three cars (compact),
    Marriage contract,
        Software in the kitchen,
Already grace the Joneses' lives, that family of vision.

Mobile daily,
    Swapping gaily,
        They VisiCalc™ their plans.
They've automated merriment and inventoried cans.

The cars, I'd say,
    Are here to stay
        Pollution notwithstanding.
Their needs to travel far and fast are simply too demanding.

Those high tech vows
    Are Mickey Spouse.
        No sooner they'd exchanged them,
Than there arose some discontent and she tried to exchange
    him.

But, ah, computer
    In the boudoir—
        Society's salvation.
It keeps that couple off the road and circumvents frustration.

Since they don't read
    Or watch TV
        But sit before the CRT,
Computer is the common bond which keeps them home and
    keeps them fond.

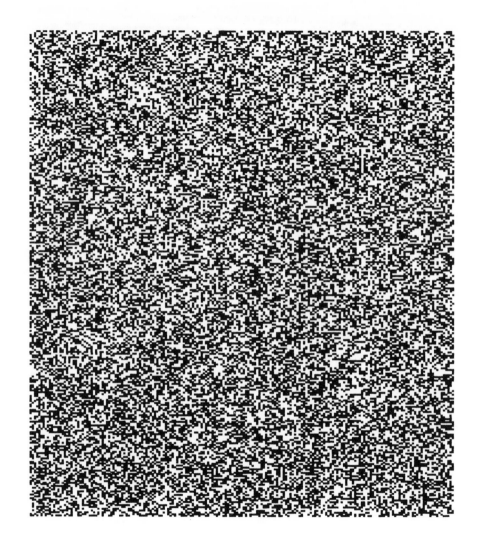

RANDOM THOUGHTS

Thought for Food

I am the Machine, and my food is thought.
I ingest your ideas, both lukewarm and hot.
I crunch up your numbers and nibble your words.
I love algorithms, though I can't stomach surds.

A sort for breakfast, a merge for lunch,
I wash it all down with some Hollerith punch.
For dinner I'm having a big Batch-B-Queue,
But dessert will be light, a file copy or two.

For a snack I might take an array's inverse,
A treat to which people seem strangely averse.
I also enjoy tasting numbers of primes,
While you make a face, as with lemons or limes.

Oh, I'm a computer. I like to eat best
Those problems you humans find tough to digest.

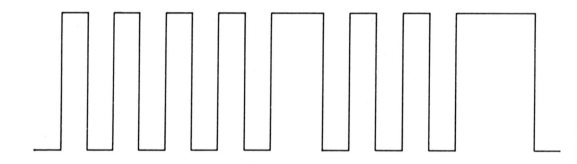

PULSE TRAIN

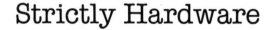

Strictly Hardware

Pulse train! Pulse train!
Where are you going again and again?
Sensed with my logic-probe ear to the ground,
Seen with oscilloscope eye once you're found.

Are you the system's clock, fast-beating heart?
Are you a serial stream from UART?
Are you out sequencing data from RAM?
Or are you just noise from a finicky fan?

Are you controlling fast access to disk,
Tidying transfers so nothing is missed?
Watching you dart as a pencil of light,
I am enthralled by your purposeful flight:

Tirelessly running the circuit board traces,
Visiting exotic switched, gated places.
Part of me resonates, kindred domain.
My brain! My brain!

Systems Surprise

So you think you know the data-flows,
Where each iota of info goes and originates.
Feels good right down to the tips of your toes,
But I've a surprise for you
      (I'm the user).

    Response time of six seconds just won't do.
    (I forgot how our clients line up in a queue.)
    You must cut response from six seconds to two.

You've charted through my office maze.
You've penetrated the murky haze of my specifications,
And through it all you've remained unfazed.
Well, I've a surprise for you
      (I'm the user).

I will need retrospectives (so sorry I'm late),
And they must be on-line since our clients can't wait.
So just change the history from one year to eight.

And now on the verge of implementation,
You no doubt feel a mild jubilation and happiness
At your elegant unified software creation.
Oh, I've a surprise for you
        (I'm the user).

I've just gone and ordered a new machine.
(The old one is dusty, the clients like clean.)
Just use the new OS, whatever that means.

Dear User, I sympathize with your requests,
But your needs for this system shall remain unmet.
My analysis shows, (by the way, I am through),
That YOU *simply don't know what it is that you* DO!

MOIRE WHEEL

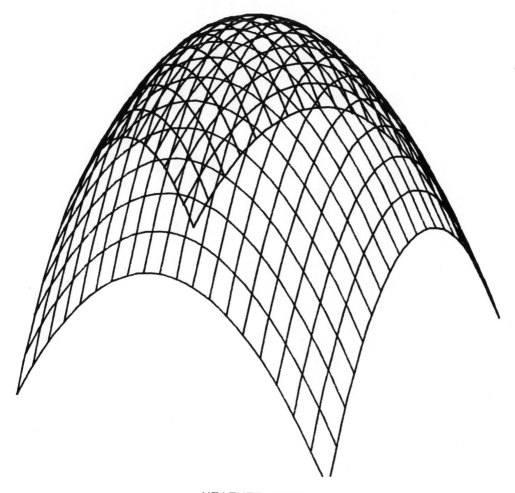

WEATHER DOME

CHAIN REACTION

60

Cottage Industry

One has his VCR-TV,
    Another has a fast MG,
        But I prefer my new PC.

While Daniel tapes from NBC,
    And Susan shines the BRG,
        I'm programming in PLC.

Recording tweaks the FTC,
    While speeding irks the CHP.
        My system's cleared the FCC.

And with my domiciled PC
    I tame huge files from A to Z
        As easily as ABC.

I market listings far and wide
    For mailings, research, and fund drives
        And sell my software on the side.

My cottage shop's no Harvard B
    But, much inspired by Visi-C,
        I'll someday make NYSE.

This Is The Tape

This is the tape
    That hung the system.

        This is the operator that mounted the tape,
        Creased the edges, then mounted the tape
            That hung the system.

This is the program that wrote on the tape
Volumes of data from invoices scraped,
Stuck now in limbo while writing the tape
That hung the system.

        This is the programmer tearing his hair,
        Thinking it his sorry onus to bear
        Having written the program which wrote to the tape
            That hung the system.

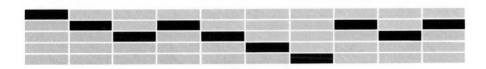

This is the user in fury, in rage,
Helplessly caught in technology's cage,
Waiting for output and looking, in vain,
For a tape neatly labeled and sealed against rain
Which, however, still sits threaded up on a drive
    Having hung the system

      And this is the system designer, whose ears
      Are blissfully distant from chaos and tears
      Caused when this trivial error appears,
      Whose lack of foresight and failure of thought
      Produced a system intol'rant to faults,
      A system which choked on the checksum result
      On the edge-crumpled tape from the treasurer's vault
      And brought the whole enterprise down to its knees
      When it looked for some sevens and came up with threes
        And hung the system.

BRIDGES, II

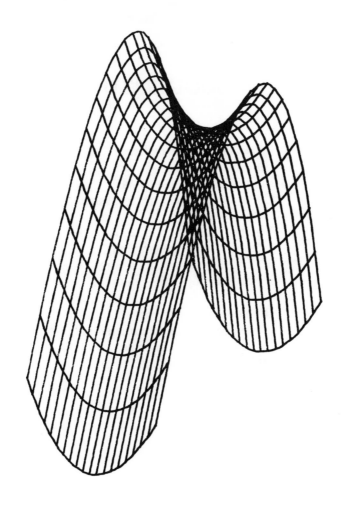

STRIP OF SPACE

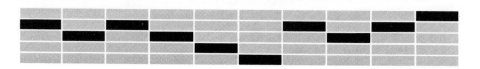

Bootstrap

Click, click, jiggle, flick.
Bootstrap loader bit-by-bit.
In the old days, just to start
Computer required dextrous art.

Binary machine commands
Are all it really understands.
To talk in English, in its core,
It needs a program—"monitor".

But how to read the program in
From disk or tape in storage bin?
Computer hadn't any clue
Of how or what it ought to do.

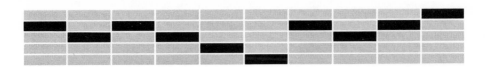

So operator at the switch
Put bootstrap loader, bit-by-bit,
Into the memory before
Machine could load the monitor.

Click, click, jiggle, flick.
The tedium could make you sick,
And if a bit got put in wrong
Computer wouldn't run for long.

No more one hears the bootstrap song,
For nowadays it's stored in ROM,
And all you do is turn it on.
Another generation gone.

Complementarity

You're a computer, and I'm a man.
The gulf between us is deep.
I don't suffer from disk contention,
Nor you from tired feet.

I don't turn off when the power fails.
You don't pay income tax,
Nor do I have a card reader to jam.
And you don't have ear wax.

I don't choke on dynamic cinch.
You don't wear a tie.
And staying awake through the midnight shift,
You *do,* I can only try.

But though we differ in many ways,
There's complementarity strong.
You calculate at lightning speed,
And I can judge right from wrong.

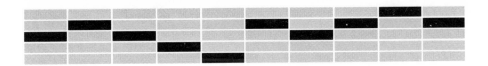

You can remember a gigabyte;
I tell you what to recall.
You can design an ultrastrong wing,
And I can design a mall.

I see the forest and you count the trees,
My vision supplemented with facts
Fetched from your database—total recall—
Something I surely lack.

I create you, and you help me think
And finish my work on time.
I also could use a little assist
IN FINISHING OFF THIS RHYME.

  (Thanks!)

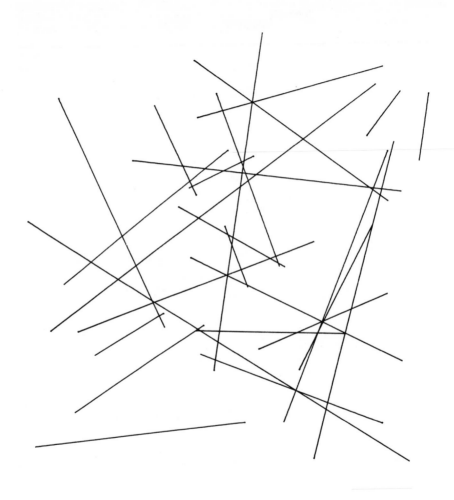

UNTITLED

TRAFFIC, NIGHT AND DAY

The Questionnaire

"I've done a survey,"
　　Revealed the user.
"Would you please put it
　　On the computer?"

I could hardly help grin at the form it was in
But required restraint not to throw it at him.

The questions were scattered all over the pages,
Aimlessly wand'ring like beasts in their cages.
Answers numerical, answers in words:
With Satan's design, it could not have been worse.

Some questions were numbered while others were not,
But the ones that were numbered were quite hard to spot
Since some answers were mindlessly numbered as well;
The whole questionnaire was chaotic as hell.

If a keypuncher had to invent a nightmare,
There's no question, it would be this questionnaire.

"Supposing we punch them,"
    I asked by design,
"What kind of analysis
    Had you mind?"

This question caught user a bit unprepared.
He squirmed like a guinea pig recently snared.
One hardly believes the response he'd in store,
"Just process them. That's what DP is for!"

```
NNNNNNNNNNNNNNNNNNNNNNNNNNNNNNNNNNNNNNNNNNNNNNNNN
NNNNNNNNNNNNNNNNNNNNNNNNNNNNNNNNNNNNNNNNNNNNNNNNN
NNNNNNNNNNNNNNNNNNNNNNNNNNNNNNNNNNNNNNNNNNNNNNNNN
NNNNNNNNNNNNNNNNNNNNNNNNNNNNNNNNNNNNNNNNNNNNNNNNN
NNNNNNNNNNNNNNNNNNNNNNNNNNNNNNNNNNNNNNNNNNNNNNNNN
ENNNNNNNNNNNNNNNNNNNNNNNNNNNNNNNNNNNNNNNNNNNNNDDDD
ENNNNNNNNNNNNNNNNNNNNNNNNNNNNNNNNNNNNNNNNNNNNNDDDD
ENNNNNNNNNNNNNNNNNNNNNNNNNNNNNNNNNNNNNNNNNNNNNDDDD
ENNNNNNNNNNNNNNNNNNNNNNNNNNNNNNNNNNNNNNNNNNNNNDDDD
ENNNNNNNNNNNNNNNNNNNNNNNNNNNNNNNNNNNNNNNNNNNNNDDDD
ENNNNNNNNNNNNNNNNNNNNNNNNNNNNNNNNNNNNNNNNNNNNNDDDD
ENNNNNNNNNNNNNNNNNNNNNNNNNNNNNNNNNNNNNNNNNNNNNDDDD
EEEEEEEEEEEEEEEEEEEEEEEEE              DDDDDDDDDDDDD
EEEEEEEEEEEEEEEEEEEEEEEEE              DDDDDDDDDDDDD
EEEEEEEEEEEEEEEEEEEEEEEEE              DDDDDDDDDDDDD
EEEEEEEEEEEEEEEEEEEEEEEEE              DDDDDDDDDDDDD
EEEEEEEEEEEEEEEEEEEEEEEEE              DDDDDDDDDDDDD
EEEEEEEEEEEEEEEEEEEEEEEEE              DDDDDDDDDDDDD
EEEEEEEEEEEEEEEEEEEEEEEEE              DDDDDDDDDDDDD
EEEEEEEEEEEEEEEEEEEEEEEEE              DDDDDDDDDDDDD
EEEEEEEEEEEEEEEEEEEEEEEEE              DDDDDDDDDDDDD
EEEEEEEEEEEEEEEEEEEEEEEEE              DDDDDDDDDDDDD
EEEEEEEEEEEEEEEEEEEEEEEEE              DDDDDDDDDDDDD
EEEEEEEEEEEEEEEEEEEEEEEEE              DDDDDDDDDDDDD
EEEEEEEEEEEEEEEEEEEEEEEEE              DDDDDDDDDDDDD
EEEEEEEEEEEEEEEEEEEEEEEEE              DDDDDDDDDDDDD
                                      DDDDDDDDDDDDD
                                      DDDDDDDDDDDDD
                                      DDDDDDDDDDDDD
                                      DDDDDDDDDDDDD
                                      DDDDDDDDDDDDD
```

END

Motivation

Not what you have, but what you are doing.
Not where you are, but where you are going.
Not your position, but your direction.
Not your "now," but what is ensuing.

Life is a process, not a thing.
Tomorrow means more than yesterday.
Life isn't a thing, but a process.

In the dark of night, you watch the stars.
You follow the waves on the ocean's face.
In the mountain's mists, you reach for a crest
And ponder the meaning of time's passing hours.

You are a person, not a machine.
Your spirit means more than your physical clay.
You're not a machine, but a person.

A Mini Glossary

address mode   addressing modes are various software techniques for fetching or storing information in the main memory of the computer.

algorithm   a step-by-step recipe for solving a problem.

APL   a programming language which employs special symbolic operators rather than Englishlike instructions.

array inverse   a mathematical operation which is exceedingly tedious when done by hand; contemporary computers do this task quickly and with minimal programming effort.

BASIC   a programming language often employed by computer hobbyists.

batch-B-queue   a queue of programs waiting to run in batch mode, that is, one after another with no contact with the user; batch programs are often given relative priorities for access to machine resources, the priorities being denoted as B, C, D, etc.

bay   a cabinet housing computer equipment.

binary   the number system employed in the internal operations of the computer.

bit   the basic unit of information which a computer can store or manipulate.

bit bucket   a register which holds the overflow from a binary operation.

board   *see* "circuit board."

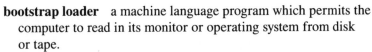

bootstrap loader a machine language program which permits the computer to read in its monitor or operating system from disk or tape.

BRG British Racing Green, a classic color for sports cars.

bubble memory a high-density information storage technology employing magnetic bubbles in a solid state medium.

buffer an area used for temporary storage in transferring data between various parts of a computer system.

bulk storage the medium for storing programs and data which are not currently active in the main memory of the computer.

bundled a computer system in which hardware and software are sold together as a package is said to be bundled.

byte a small unit of information storage: eight bits, the amount needed to store one character, such as a letter or digit.

capacitive keyboard a touch-sensitive keyboard which has no moving parts.

card another term for a circuit board; or, a punched card for data transfer.

card image a file which is stored on disk or tape just as it would appear in punched cards, without any reformatting.

checksum a method of detecting errors on a tape in which, after a block of data is written on the tape, the computer calculates the sum of the data and writes this as a checksum on the tape; later, when the tape is read, the computer recalculates the sum and checks it against the checksum on the tape.

chip   a small piece of solid-state material from which integrated circuits are fabricated.

CHP   California Highway Patrol.

circuit board   circuit boards contain sockets and interconnections for the integrated circuits and other electronic components from which computers are built.

clock   the inner workings of the CPU and its interactions with other components of the computer are coordinated by a "clock" which produces a steady train of accurately timed pulses; this clock operates typically at a rate of several million pulses per second, giving the computer its remarkable speed.

COBOL   a programming language used for business applications; COBOL has hundreds of different instructions.

code   a term for a computer program.

compile   compilation is the process of translating a computer program into the binary machine instructions which the computer can execute; a program which carries out the translation process is called a compiler.

core   a term for the main memory of a computer.

CPU   central processing unit, the "nerve center" of a computer.

CRT   "cathode-ray tube" terminal, a televisionlike computer terminal.

data-flows   the paths of information interchange identified in a systems analysis of an application problem, such as library circulation, bank transactions, etc.

DIM   the instruction for allocating data arrays in BASIC.

disk   information storage technology employing rotating magnetic disks; rigid or "hard" disks provide large capacity and very fast access; flexible or "floppy" disks have smaller capacity and are slower but are less costly than hard disks.

documentation   explanatory material which accompanies a computer program.

DP   data processing.

drive, disk or tape   the device which reads and writes data using a magnetic disk or tape medium.

dynamic cinch   a defect in a magnetic tape caused by incorrect tension from the tape-drive motors.

END   the keyword used to signal the physical end of a program in BASIC and certain other programming languages.

engineering   the professional area dealing with the design of computer hardware (as used here); one may also speak of "software engineering," referring to the systematic (as opposed to haphazard) design, refinement, and testing of large computer programs.

enhance   modifications to software or hardware are termed "enhancements," regardless of whether performance is actually improved.

FCC   Federal Communications Commission; the FCC has set a standard limiting radio and TV interference from personal computers; some early PC's did not meet this standard.

firmware   *see* "ROM."

FOR/NEXT   the construction for setting up loops in BASIC.

FTC   Federal Trade Commission.

gated   gates are basic switching units of digital circuits.

gigabyte   a large unit of data storage—one billion bytes.

hard disk   *see* "disk."

hardware   the tangible, "nuts and bolts" of a computer system—the cabinets, power supplies, and electronic components.

Harvard B   Harvard Graduate School of Business; *see* "VisiCalc™."

hex(adecimal)   a number system sometimes employed in computers, in which binary bits are manipulated in groups of four.

Hollerith   the standard coding scheme used for representing data on punched cards.

IC   integrated circuit; a solid-state electronic device containing hundreds, thousands, or hundreds of thousands of binary switching elements integrated into one "chip."

IF THEN   the construction for decision-making in programs written in BASIC and certain other languages.

I/O   the input/output portion of a computer or computer system.

keypunch method of data entry in which data are punched into cards and then read into the computer via a card reader.

language, programming the communication vehicle via which instructions are given to the computer; the computer's intrinsic binary instruction set is "machine language;" higher level programming languages more amenable to human activity must be interpreted or compiled into machine language in order for the computer to execute the instructions.

LET the instruction for assigning values to variables in BASIC.

logic-probe a device for detecting electronic states and pulses in digital circuits.

machine language *see* "language."

mainframe a large computer system designed to handle the most demanding computational tasks and large numbers of users; mainframe computers range in cost from about $500,000 to many millions of dollars.

main memory *see* "RAM."

maintenance programming a programming task in which, rather than creating new programs, the programmer seeks to upgrade and improve existing programs which may have cost enormous sums of money to develop.

MAT the keyword for carrying out matrix or array operations in some dialects of BASIC.

megabyte a large unit of data storage—one million bytes.

merge *see* "sort/merge."

microcomputer a computer in which the CPU is fabricated on one integrated circuit; once implying rather limited computational capacity, the term "microcomputer" now includes machines whose power vies with traditional minicomputers.

minicomputer a medium capacity computer designed to handle several users (say, 4 to 60); this has become a somewhat nebulous classification: some current minicomputers ("superminis") are comparable in computational power with traditional mainframe computers, while some current microcomputers compete with traditional minis.

MIPS million-instructions-per-second; a measure of the operating speed of a CPU.

modes *see* "address mode."

monitor also called the operating system, a master supervisory program which manages the computer's resources and allows the user to communicate in something other than primitive binary numbers.

nested loop a software construction in which a repetitive sequence of instructions is nested inside another reptitive sequence, which may be nested inside another repetitive sequence, and so on.

Neumann John von Neumann conceived the idea of a stored-program computer; this represented, in essence, the invention of computer software.

NYSE New York Stock Exchange.

octal   a number system sometimes employed in computers, in which
binary digits are manipulated in groups of three.

operations   the professional area concerned with the day-to-day care
and feeding of medium to large computer systems; operators
mount tapes, regulate the work flow to the computer, distribute
printouts, and so forth.

OS   operating system, the master supervisory program which
manages a computer's resources.

oscilloscope   a piece of test equipment used for troubleshooting
computers and other electronic devices; it makes visible rapidly
changing voltage patterns.

overflow   the condition in which the result of a binary operation
exceeds the numeric capacity of the machine, thereby generating
an extra bit which may, in some computers, be trapped in a one-bit
register or "bit bucket."

parallel processor   a processing unit which can carry out more than
one operation at a time; the human right brain shows some parallel
processing characteristics.

Pascal   a recently developed programming language which enforces
the discipline of structured programming and other good
programming practices.

PC   personal computer.

PL/1   a programming language which incorporates features of
FORTRAN and COBOL, attempting to provide broad capability
for both numeric and nonnumeric applications.

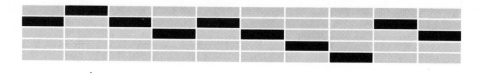

PLC a version of the programming language PL/1 designed to run on microcomputers.

prime number a number which cannot be evenly divided by any number other than itself and 1; the search for ever larger prime numbers has intrigued mathematicians for centuries and has become a challenge for computer people; the current record for the largest prime is held by two high-school students who used several thousand hours of computer time on a very fast computer in pursuit of their goal.

programming the professional area which deals with the preparation of the lists of instructions called computer programs; the vocabulary for the instructions is determined by the choice of programming language—BASIC, Pascal, SNOBOL, etc.

pulse train a sequence of electronic pulses characteristic of digital circuitry.

RAM random-access memory, the main memory in which the computer stores programs and data in active use.

recursive the characteristic of defining something in terms of itself; contemporary programming languages often provide the capability for defining recursive functions.

relational database a type of database organization which allows very flexible retrieval of data.

release each successive version of a piece of software is termed a "release."

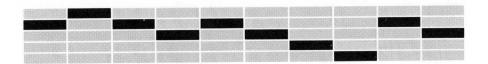

REM   the keyword for remarks or comments in a program written in BASIC; also, rapid-eye-movement, a stage of sleep.

response time   a measure of computer performance: the time elapsed between a user's issuing a command and the computer's delivery of the associated response.

RETURN   the keyword which marks the end of a subroutine in BASIC and other programming languages.

ROM   read-only memory, an integrated circuit which has a program permanently stored in it; a ROM, thus, is both hardware and software and is sometimes referred to as "firmware."

schema   the formal organization of a computer database.

'scope   *see* "oscilloscope."

sequential processor   a processing unit which carries out instructions one-at-a-time in sequence; the human left brain shows some sequential processing characteristics.

servo   an electromechanical device used for controlling, for example, the rotation speed of a disk.

software   computer programs.

solid state   the switching technology exemplified by transistors and integrated circuits, in which the circuit elements are fabricated on small pieces of solid semiconductor material or "chips."

sort/merge   a standard computer procedure for updating a file, in which a sorted list of new transactions is merged with an existing master file.

spelling checker   a component of a word processing system which checks the spelling in a piece of text against a stored dictionary of tens of thousands of words and flags any discrepancies.

structured programming   a formal programming discipline which, among its characteristics, encourages the use of bounded control structures, such as WHILE/DO and REPEAT/UNTIL and eschews the unconditional branch GOTO.

subroutine   a section of a computer program which handles a specific processing task and can be invoked by other parts of the program when needed, returning to the main program when the task is completed.

surd   an irrational number, such as the square root of 2, which cannot be represented as a ratio of whole numbers.

swapping scheme   a software component which mediates the sharing of a computer by several simultaneous users.

tenth-inch centers   the standard spacing for the holes in circuit boards into which the integrated circuits are inserted.

traces   the conductors which interconnect the various electronic components on a circuit board.

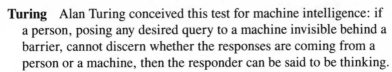

Turing Alan Turing conceived this test for machine intelligence: if a person, posing any desired query to a machine invisible behind a barrier, cannot discern whether the responses are coming from a person or a machine, then the responder can be said to be thinking.

typing a programming language is said to be "strongly typed" if it checks for errors based on the programmer's declaration of the uses to be made of variables in the program.

UART "universal asynchronous receiver/transmitter", an integrated circuit used for input/output functions in computers and terminals.

user the ultimate beneficiary of the efforts of computer professionals—"we do it all for users"; users range from individuals who know nothing about computers to those with a sophisticated appreciation of a system's subtleties.

VCR video cassette recorder.

VisiCalc™ a program to aid in budgeting and other "spreadsheet" applications; a great software success, over 300,000 copies of VisiCalc™ were sold in its first three years; the creator was a first-year graduate student at Harvard Business School.

Index of Major Themes